ELEPHANT SEAL ISLAND

by Evelyn Shaw
Pictures by Cherryl Pape

A Science I CAN READ Book

Harper & Row, Publishers
New York, Hagerstown, San Francisco, London

FIRST EDITION

Library of Congress Cataloging in Publication Data
Shaw, Evelyn S.
  Elephant seal island.

  (A Science I can read book)
  SUMMARY: Describes the cyclical visitations of
elephant seals to Año Nuevo Island in the
Pacific Ocean and relates the experiences of a
male pup from birth to early adulthood.
  1. Elephant seals—Juvenile literature.
[1. Elephant seals.   2. Seals (Animals)]
I. Pape, Cherryl.   II. Title.
QL737.P64S5 1978   599'.748   77-25649
ISBN 0-06-025603-6
ISBN 0-06-025604-4 lib. bdg.

To my dear friend, Arlene Tucker-Levin

It is a cold day

in November.

The sun hides

behind dark gray clouds.

5

The wind makes the ocean
white and foamy.
Big waves
crash onto a small island.

6

The island is in

the Pacific Ocean.

It is called Año Nuevo.

Sea gulls and sea lions

sit on the rocks.

The sandy beach is empty.

Soon a big wave rolls

onto the beach.

A large animal

falls onto the sand.

It is a male elephant seal.

He is fourteen feet long.

He has flippers for swimming.

He cannot walk on them.

He drags his body

across the sandy beach.

Soon another elephant seal
comes out of the ocean.
And another, and another.
Now fifty elephant seals
rest on the beach.
All these seals are males.

They are called bulls.

Each year, in November,

bulls come to this island.

They wait for the females.

The bulls wait to mate.

Old bulls are bigger

than young bulls.

The noses of old bulls

are bigger

than the noses of young bulls.

14

Bulls chase and push each other.

They make loud noises

through their large noses.

Sometimes,

bulls bite each other.

A fight ends

when one bull moves away.

The smaller bull

usually loses the fight.

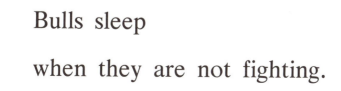

Bulls sleep

when they are not fighting.

17

One month passes.

Now it is December.

The females arrive.

One, two, twenty,

two hundred females

come out of the ocean.

They are smaller than bulls.

They have smaller noses.

Soon the females give birth

to pups.

A pup is born to each female.

One female is bigger

than the others.

The scientists

who are watching the seals

name her Rita.

They spray her name on her

with hair dye.

Rita is six years old.

She gives birth to a male pup.

The scientists name him Basil.

They put a tag on his flipper.

Later they will spray

his name on him.

Basil is black and shiny,

long and skinny.

He has large flippers.

Basil is born hungry.

He weighs about fifty pounds.

He wants to suck milk.

He looks for a nipple

on Rita's big belly.

It takes Basil an hour

to find a nipple.

He sucks milk from his mother.

23

Basil sucks lots of milk every day.

He gains ten pounds every day.

He grows very fat.

At three weeks

Basil weighs 250 pounds!

One morning

Basil gets lost

behind a big female.

26

Rita cannot see him.

She hunts for him.

Rita sees a pup.

All pups look alike.

They do not smell alike.

Rita smells the pup.

It does not smell like Basil.

Rita makes a loud noise.

EEGGHH.

Then she bites the pup.

The pup cries.

Her mother hears her.

She is angry.

She makes a loud noise, too.

EEGGHH.

She fights with Rita.

Rita is bigger.

She wins the fight.

Rita is tired of looking

for Basil.

She goes to sleep.

A hungry pup sees Rita sleeping.

He sucks milk from her nipple.

Then Basil sees Rita.

He is hungry too.

Pups are always hungry.

Now two pups are sucking.

Rita wakes up.

She smells both pups.

She turns to bite

the visiting pup.

That pup drags itself away.

Basil naps near his mother.

Suddenly

Basil hears Rita screaming.

A big bull is rushing

to Rita.

Other females move out of his way.

Some pups do not move

out of his way fast enough.

They are squashed to death

under his body.

The big bull

pushes Basil away.

Basil cries to be
near his mother.
The bull
mates with Rita.
Then he leaves.

Basil goes back to his mother.

He is happy

to suck some milk.

At four weeks

Basil weighs almost 350 pounds!

He is very, very fat.

Now Basil is fat enough

for his mother to leave him.

38

Early one morning

Basil is fast asleep.

Rita moves down

to the ocean.

She swims away from the island.

Next year in December

she will come back.

Then she will give birth

to a new pup.

She will mate.

But Basil will never see her again.

His mother is gone.

When Basil wakes up

he screams.

He is very hungry.

He has no mother.

He has no milk.

All the other mothers

have gone back to the ocean.

All the bulls have gone, too.

Only pups are left

on the island.

Basil drags himself

over to the other pups.

They are all very fat.

They have silvery fur.

The pups are called weaners

because they do not nurse anymore.

Weaners stay on the island

for two more months.

During that time

they do not eat.

They become thinner.

Every morning

weaners drag their bodies

down to the edge of the ocean.

Basil goes with them.

At first he dunks

in little pools of water.

He splashes in the water.

He does not put his face in.

He learns about many things.

He smells seaweed and rocks.

He watches flying birds.

On the beach

weaners play with each other.

They raise their heads.

They pretend to fight.

Sometimes they fall

and roll down the beach.

As the days pass

the weaners get bolder.

Basil gets bolder, too.

He puts his face in the water.

He moves into deeper water.

He floats.

He teaches himself

how to swim and dive.

He does not have a mother or father

to teach him.

When he is three months old,

Basil is ready to leave the island.

All the weaners are ready

to live in the ocean.

One by one

they swim away.

They must learn

to catch their own fish food.

They must watch for killer whales.

Killer whales eat

baby elephant seals.

Sharks eat baby elephant seals.

Some weaners do not escape

from them.

Some weaners do not learn

to catch fish very well.

They starve to death.

Basil catches lots of fish

in the ocean.

But he cannot stay
underwater all the time.
He is not a fish.
He is a mammal
that lives in the ocean.
Mammals breathe air.
Basil must put his nose out
to breathe in the air.

Years pass.

Now Basil is a young bull.

He is seven years old.

He is big.

He is ready to mate

with the females.

In November

Basil goes to the island

where he was born.

He goes back

to Año Nuevo.

The scientists mark him again.

He waits on the beach

until the females come.

Meanwhile,

he pushes and chases other bulls.

He will do this every year

for many years.

He will mate with many females.

Basil may be the father

of 100 elephant seals.